DATE DUE

5-10-07			

A g C
O m k
O R L
e
w

Published by Creative Education
123 South Broad Street, Mankato, Minnesota 56001

Creative Education is an imprint of The Creative Company.
Design by Stephanie Blumenthal
Art direction by Rita Marshall

Photographs by Corbis (Lucian Aigner, Nathan Benn, Bettmann, Burstein Collection, Robert Farber, Natalie Fobes, Cynthia Hart
Designer, Historical Picture Archive, Eric and David Hosking, Allen Kennedy, Francis G. Mayer, Mosaic Image, Michael Nicholson,
John Sparks), Getty Images (Photodisc)

Library of Congress Cataloging-in-Publication Data

Fandel, Jennifer.
Rhyme, meter, and other word music / by Jennifer Fandel.
p. cm. — (Understanding poetry)
Includes index.
ISBN 978-1-58341-342-5
1. Poetics—Juvenile literature. 2. Rhyme—Juvenile literature. 3. Versification—Juvenile
literature. I. Title. II. Understanding poetry (Mankato, Minn.)

PN1059.R5F36 2005
808.1—dc22   2004058230

4 6 8 9 7 5 3

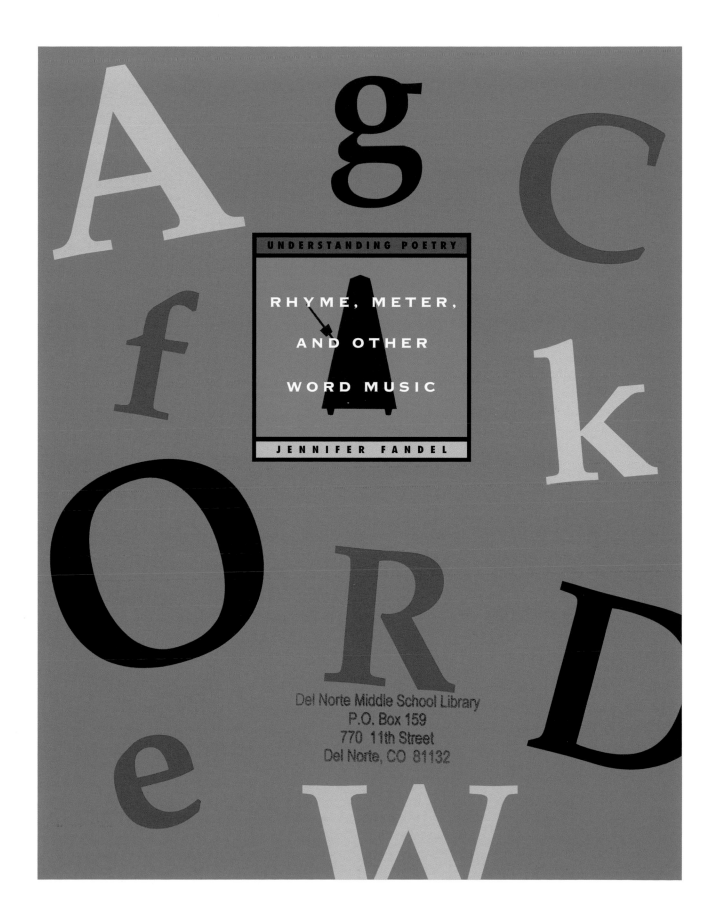

UNDERSTANDING POETRY

RHYME, METER, AND OTHER WORD MUSIC

JENNIFER FANDEL

CREATIVE 🍎 EDUCATION

A car drives down the street, its stereo blaring. The drums thump, and the beat captures you. You shuffle your feet as you walk. You hum tunes under the light of the moon. And then you stop. Listen. Hear the cool wind sighing through the trees. Hear the call of an owl echoing through the night. Hear the rumble of thunder or the hush of a steady rain. Music is all around you. You hear it in nature, listen to it on the radio, and create it with your actions and voice. Poetry captures this music with its echoes, beats, and sounds.

Poetry began as an oral, or spoken, art form. Long ago, before books were widely available, poetry was often recited and sung. A **minstrel** would sing the poem for a group of listeners, sometimes playing a small, hand-held harp at the same time. The audience often joined in the singing, and many times the particular **rhyme** or **rhythm** of the poem would stick in their minds. Doing their work in the fields or at home, people would recall the music of the poetry they had heard, rather than the actual letters and words written on a page. People

4

long ago recognized that much of poetry's power and beauty came through the music they heard when the words were spoken or sung.

Poetry's **oral tradition** is still alive today. While we are used to seeing poetry typed on a page, we are still expected to hear the poem when we are reading. Without the music of poetry, many poems would simply be a collection of words and images. The sound, rhyme, rhythm, and **meter** of a poem give it shape and form. In addition, the music helps you hear the voices and experience the emotions of a poem. Music invites you in. It surrounds you as you read and write. It breathes. It dances. And it lingers in your memory, waiting for the right word or image to bring the music back to life again.

THE CHIME OF RHYME

When your parents or other adults read to you as a child, they probably began with nursery rhymes such as "Humpty Dumpty" and "The Old Woman Who Lived in a Shoe." You probably listened and clapped along to the music of the poems, enjoying the rhymes that fell at the end of each line. Long ago, when people sang their poems, they had an easier time remembering the words if they used rhymes, particularly end rhymes. End rhymes are rhymes that fall at the ends of lines; for example, "Humpty Dumpty sat on a wall. Humpty Dumpty had a great fall."

American poet Robert Frost (1874–1963) was a master of end rhyming and used it frequently in his poems. The memorable rhymes and rhythm in "Stopping by Woods on a Snowy Evening" make this poem fairly easy to memorize. Give it a try!

STOPPING BY WOODS ON A SNOWY EVENING

Whose woods these are I think I know.
His house is in the village though;
He will not see me stopping here
To watch his woods fill up with snow.

My little horse must think it queer
To stop without a farmhouse near
Between the woods and frozen lake
The darkest evening of the year.

He gives his harness bells a shake
To ask if there is some mistake.
The only other sound's the sweep
Of easy wind and downy flake.

The woods are lovely, dark and deep,
But I have promises to keep,
And miles to go before I sleep,
And miles to go before I sleep.

The end rhymes that Frost uses are known as perfect rhymes. The words rhyme exactly, meaning their vowel sounds and end consonant sounds are the same. In the case of "shake/mistake/flake," we see that all of the words have a long a sound and end in a hard k sound. You'll notice, though, that all perfect rhymes aren't spelled the same way. Though and snow are perfect rhymes because they contain the same sounds, even though they are spelled differently.

If you look at poetry written today, you'll notice that much of it doesn't use perfect end rhymes. Some poets think that perfect end rhymes take the surprise and freshness out of a poem. They believe this because some poems, such as the ones you often find in greeting cards, sound sing-songy and may use odd words or strange word combinations to force a line to rhyme. The best rhymes usually sound natural, meaning that the words seem to fit well with the rest of the poem. Poets who avoid perfect end rhyme often still use rhyme, but they use two other types of rhyme: slant rhyme and internal rhyme.

American poet Emily Dickinson (1830–86) was known for her use of slant rhyme. Slant rhymes are rhymes that sound similar but aren't as closely matched as perfect rhymes. They may use similar vowel sounds and different endings, such as **red** and **wedding**, or different vowel sounds and the same ending, such as **stop** and **step**. You can see a good example of slant rhyme in Dickinson's poem "I Heard a Fly Buzz When I Died," sometimes referred to as poem number "465," since Dickinson never titled her poems.

465

I heard a Fly buzz—when I died—
The Stillness in the Room
Was like the Stillness in the Air—
Between the Heaves of Storm—

The Eyes around—had wrung them dry—
And Breaths were gathering firm
For that last Onset—when the King
Be witnessed—in the Room—

I willed my Keepsakes—Signed away
What portion of me be
Assignable—and then it was
There interposed a Fly—

With Blue—uncertain stumbling Buzz—
Between the light—and me—
And then the Windows failed—and then
I could not see to see—

Notice that many of the words at the ends of the lines have some similarities. In the first stanza, the m sounds in room and storm echo off each other, creating a slant rhyme. In the second and third stanzas, "dry / away / Fly" are slant rhymes. But in the last stanza, Dickinson uses a perfect rhyme: me and see. Some may say Dickinson's choice to use slant rhyme in the first three stanzas made the perfect rhyme in her last stanza more powerful. What do you think? Does her perfect rhyme sound out of place, or does it sound natural?

When rhymes appear in the middle of lines, they're called internal rhymes. Internal rhymes still allow you to use rhyme, but you put your rhymes in unexpected places within the poem. You might say or write "I feel my bones alone in my skin." The internal rhyme "bones / alone" gives the poem an element of surprise—right in the middle of the line.

You have a lot of choices when it comes to using rhyme, including the choice not to use it. Rhyme can help you emphasize certain sounds and rhythms, making your poem sound more musical or—in some cases—memorable.

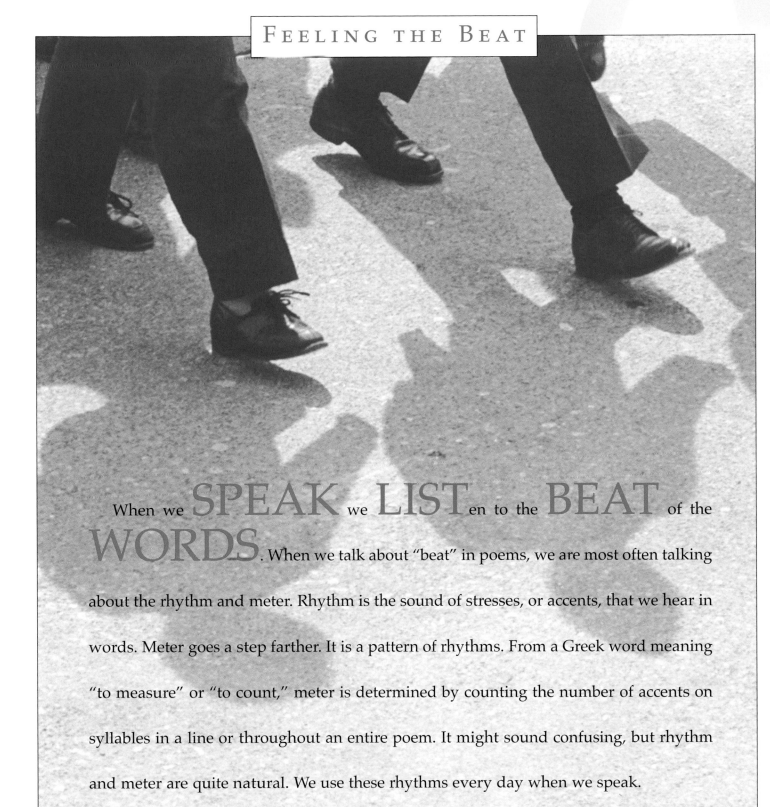

When we SPEAK we LISTen to the BEAT of the WORDS. When we talk about "beat" in poems, we are most often talking about the rhythm and meter. Rhythm is the sound of stresses, or accents, that we hear in words. Meter goes a step farther. It is a pattern of rhythms. From a Greek word meaning "to measure" or "to count," meter is determined by counting the number of accents on syllables in a line or throughout an entire poem. It might sound confusing, but rhythm and meter are quite natural. We use these rhythms every day when we speak.

There are many types of rhythm, and they all have different names. The most common rhythm in the English language is the iamb, which is often called the "heartbeat rhythm," because it makes a **bum-BUM** sound, just like a beating heart. This means that the accent is on the second syllable of a word, as in the word "today" (to-DAY). Iambs can have many different effects on a poem. Because they are so common in everyday speech, they can make a poem sound conversational. But when iambs appear repeatedly in a poem,

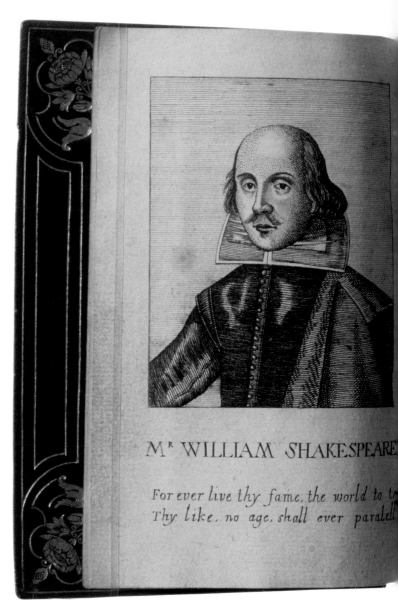

Mᴿ WILLIAM SHAKESPEARE

For ever live thy fame. the world to t̶
Thy like. no age. shall ever paralell

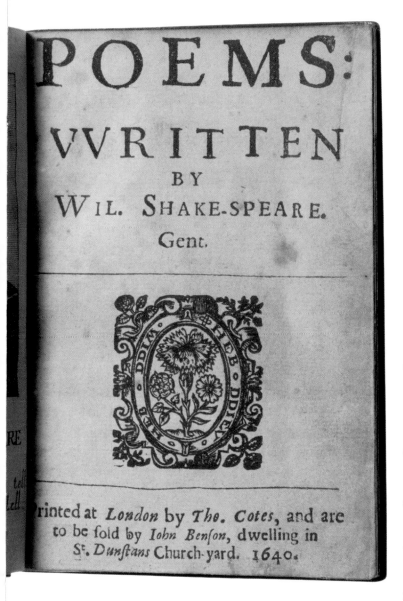

they produce a steady beat, similar to the rhythm of marching or walking. The steady rhythm of iambs can be heard in Robert Frost's poem "Stopping by Woods on a Snowy Evening" (see page 7).

If the accent is moved to the first syllable, you have a trochee. This BUM-bum rhythm can be heard in the word "thunder" (THUN-der). Trochees, whose name comes from a Greek word meaning "running," are often used within a line of iambs to break up a rhythm that sounds too repetitive.

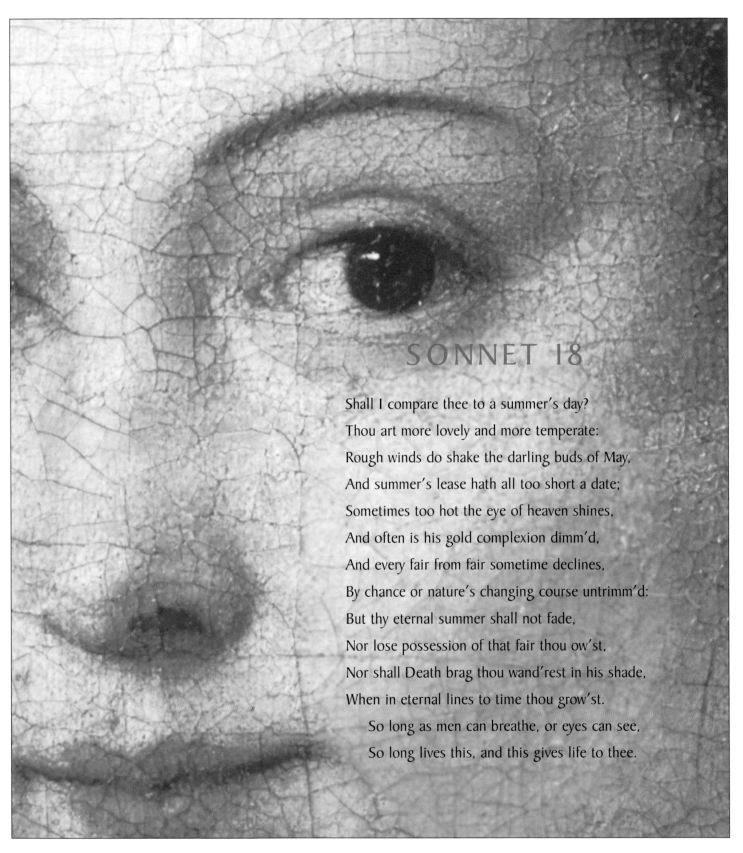

SONNET 18

Shall I compare thee to a summer's day?
Thou art more lovely and more temperate:
Rough winds do shake the darling buds of May,
And summer's lease hath all too short a date;
Sometimes too hot the eye of heaven shines,
And often is his gold complexion dimm'd,
And every fair from fair sometime declines,
By chance or nature's changing course untrimm'd:
But thy eternal summer shall not fade,
Nor lose possession of that fair thou ow'st,
Nor shall Death brag thou wand'rest in his shade,
When in eternal lines to time thou grow'st.
    So long as men can breathe, or eyes can see,
    So long lives this, and this gives life to thee.

Some meters come naturally to poets as they write, and others require a lot of work. Experimenting with meter can be both fun and challenging. Most meters are used in special poetic forms, such as the limerick and sonnet. Rhythms, though, are a natural part of the way we talk. Being aware of the rhythms of your words can help you write stronger poems. If you choose your words just right, a poem can sing, march, surprise, or even laugh on the page.

The sonnet is a form of poetry that developed in the 13th century, and poets still challenge themselves to write sonnets today. Meaning "little song," a sonnet is 14 lines long and follows a certain **rhyme scheme**. A rhyme scheme is the pattern of end rhymes in a poem, which is usually noted by letters. For example, Shakespeare's "Sonnet 18" uses this rhyme scheme: abab cdcd efef gg. Turn back to page 16 and notice that the last word of the first line, day, rhymes with the last word of the third line, May. These are noted as a in the rhyme scheme because they are the first rhymes in the poem. Similarly, temperate, at the end of the second line, rhymes with date, at the end of the fourth line. These rhymes are noted as b. The other rhymes are noted in a similar way.

Another popular poetic form is the villanelle. The villanelle has 19 lines, some of which repeat. Many people think the repeating lines make the villanelle sound like a song with a main verse, or refrain. As you read the villanelle "The Waking," by American poet Theodore Roethke (1908–63), pay attention to how the meaning of the repeating lines seems to change and grow.

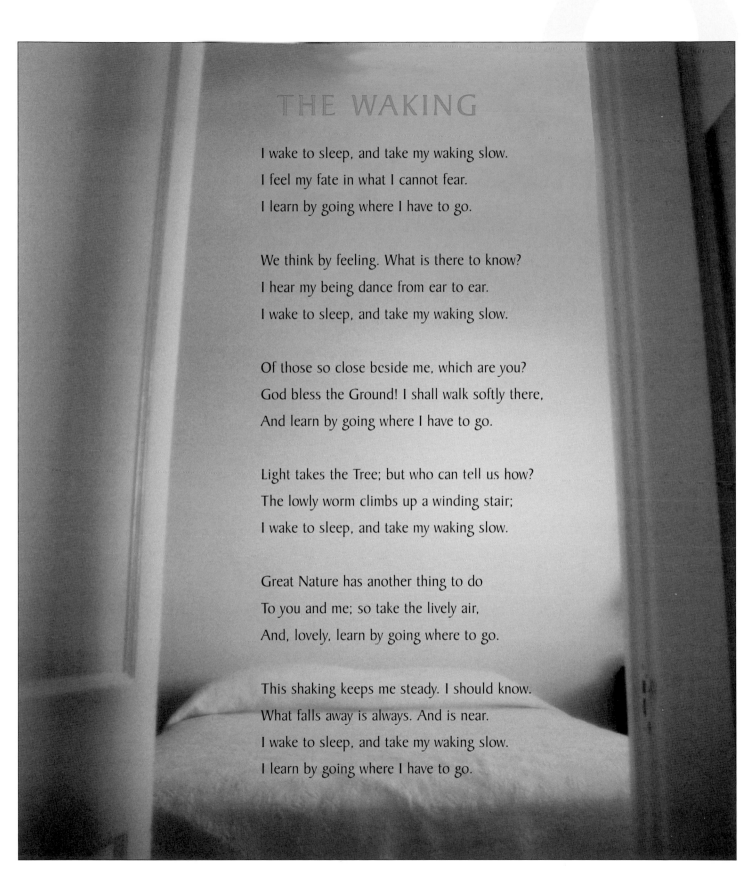

THE WAKING

I wake to sleep, and take my waking slow.
I feel my fate in what I cannot fear.
I learn by going where I have to go.

We think by feeling. What is there to know?
I hear my being dance from ear to ear.
I wake to sleep, and take my waking slow.

Of those so close beside me, which are you?
God bless the Ground! I shall walk softly there,
And learn by going where I have to go.

Light takes the Tree; but who can tell us how?
The lowly worm climbs up a winding stair;
I wake to sleep, and take my waking slow.

Great Nature has another thing to do
To you and me; so take the lively air,
And, lovely, learn by going where to go.

This shaking keeps me steady. I should know.
What falls away is always. And is near.
I wake to sleep, and take my waking slow.
I learn by going where I have to go.

Both beginning and long-time poets enjoy working with forms. Some use forms to challenge themselves, similar to doing a difficult crossword puzzle. Some find working with forms fun, because they push poets to write in a way that is different from their normal habits and discover new things about language. And there are others who find writing in forms quite natural because certain forms work well with their subject matter or approach to the poem. Give forms a try. You'll discover new things about poetry, language, and the music poems can make.

FREE-FLYING VERSE

The majority of poems written in America since the 1950s have been in **free verse**. Hearing the words "free verse" often makes people imagine that these poems are crazy, wild poems that don't follow any rules. However, because language relies on certain rules to make sense, a poem can never be free from all rules. In most cases, free verse means that a poem wasn't written in any known form, such as the sonnet. It may use rhythm, meter, and rhyme, but it typically doesn't follow any strict patterns like form poetry does.

Walt Whitman (1819–92) was one of the first American poets to begin writing in free verse. Many of his poems contain long lines with some repeating phrases, and they sound very casual, almost as if the poet is speaking rather than writing. Take a look at the following excerpt from Whitman's poem "Out of the Cradle Endlessly Rocking."

Out of the cradle endlessly rocking,

Out of the mocking-bird's throat, the musical shuttle,

Out of the Ninth-month midnight,

Over the sterile sands and the fields beyond, where the child leaving his bed wander'd
    alone, bareheaded, barefoot,

Down from the shower'd halo,

Up from the mystic play of shadows twining and twisting as if they were alive,

Out from the patches of briers and blackberries,

From the memories of the bird that chanted to me,

From your memories sad brother, from the fitful risings and fallings I heard

From under that yellow half-moon late-risen and swollen as if with tears,

From those beginning notes of yearning and love there in the mist,

From the thousand responses of my heart never to cease,

From the myriad thence-arous'd words,

From the word stronger and more delicious than any,

From such as now they start the scene revisiting,

As a flock, twittering, rising, or overhead passing,

Borne hither, ere all eludes me, hurriedly,

A man, yet by these tears a little boy again,

Throwing myself on the sand, confronting the waves,

I, chanter of pains and joys, uniter of here and hereafter,

Taking all hints to use them, but swiftly leaping beyond them,

A reminiscence sing.

In this poem, Whitman presents a long list of places before finally mentioning his subject at the end of the **stanza**. Even though Whitman doesn't follow a form in his poem, he does use rhythm and repeating words to involve readers in the chanting music of the poem. How does the rhythm and repetition affect you as you read?

By copying the rhythm, rhyme, and repeating lines used in blues music, African-American poet Langston Hughes (1902–67) was able to bring the music of the blues into his free-verse poem "The Weary Blues." Be sure to read the poem aloud to get the full effect. Do you notice any patterns in his rhythm and repeating lines? What's the effect of his rhyme, rhythm, and repeating lines on the message and feeling of the poem?

THE WEARY BLUES

Droning a drowsy syncopated tune,
Rocking back and forth to a mellow croon,
   I heard a Negro play.
Down on Lenox Avenue the other night
By the pale dull pallor of an old gas light
   He did a lazy sway. . . .
   He did a lazy sway. . . .
To the tune o' those Weary Blues.
With his ebony hands on each ivory key
He made that poor piano moan with melody.
   O Blues!
Swaying to and fro on his rickety stool
He played that sad raggy tune like a musical fool.
   Sweet Blues!
Coming from a black man's soul.
   O Blues!
In a deep song voice with a melancholy tone
I heard that Negro sing, that old piano moan—

"Ain't got nobody in all this world,
Ain't got nobody but ma self.
I's gwine to quit ma frownin'
And put ma troubles on the shelf."
Thump, thump, thump, went his foot on the floor.
He played a few chords then he sang some more—
   "I got the Weary Blues
And I can't be satisfied.
Got the Weary Blues
And can't be satisfied—
I ain't happy no mo'
And I wish that I had died."
And far into the night he crooned that tune.
   The stars went out and so did the moon.
   The singer stopped playing and went to bed
   While the Weary Blues echoed through his head.
   He slept like a rock or a man that's dead.

After Whitman, free verse became more and more popular. Many poets, starting with the **Modern** poets of the early 1900s, chose to work in free verse because they felt that forms were too artificial, traditional, and orderly. They wanted their poetry to seem natural and imperfect, much like human speech. Additionally, many poets believed forms represented old ways of doing things. These poets, excited by the possibilities of the 20th century, chose free verse because they felt its "newness" represented the new century.

Of course, it's impossible to show every type of free verse poem. E. E. Cummings (1894–1962) got rid of punctuation in his poems, used lowercase letters, and broke many words into syllables. By breaking grammar rules in extreme ways, he inspired many poets to follow. You can see some of these broken rules in the poem "[i am accused of tending to the past]," by **contemporary** African-American poet Lucille Clifton (1936–).

X

[i am accused of tending to the past]

i am accused of tending to the past
as if i made it,
as if i sculpted it
with my own hands. i did not.
this past was waiting for me
when i came,
a monstrous unnamed baby,
and i with my mother's itch
took it to breast
and named it
History.
she is more human now,
learning language everyday,
remembering faces, names and dates.
when she is strong enough to travel
on her own, beware, she will.

Alliteration, **consonance**, and **assonance** all focus on the repetition of a consonant or vowel. Alliteration is the repetition of consonants at the beginning of words, such as the repetition of the letter b in Billy busted broncos.

Consonance is the repetition of consonants at both the beginning and end of words. It's often seen in slant rhymes, such as drop / drip or falls / feels. Assonance is the repetition of vowel sounds, such as the long o sound in the yellow smoke rose.

To see alliteration, consonance, and assonance in action, let's look at the poem "The Lake Isle of Innisfree," by Irish poet William Butler Yeats (1865–1939).

THE LAKE ISLE OF INNISFREE

I will arise and go now, and go to Innisfree,
    And a small cabin build there, of clay and wattles made;
Nine bean rows will I have there, a hive for the honey bee,
    And live alone in the bee-loud glade.

And I shall have some peace there, for peace comes dropping slow,
    Dropping from the veils of the morning to where the cricket sings;
There midnight's all a glimmer, and noon a purple glow,
    And evening full of the linnet's wings.

I will arise and go now, for always night and day
    I hear lake water lapping with low sounds by the shore;
While I stand on the roadway, or on the pavements gray,
    I hear it in the deep heart's core.

This poem celebrates a place of relaxation for Yeats, and the sounds in the poem help readers step into that calm, relaxed state. The sounds you hear are of nature, of water lapping and crickets singing. In the line "I hear lake water lapping with low sounds by the shore," Yeats uses alliteration, focusing on the l sound. He also uses assonance in this line with his frequent use of the long O sound. Both of these sounds together make readers feel soothed. Can you find other patterns of alliteration and assonance in Yeats's poem? How do these sounds make you feel as you read?

Another sound tool that poets often love to use is **onomatopoeia** (on-uh-mot-uh-PEE-uh). This long Greek word means "name making," and a word is said to be onomatopoetic when its name resembles the sound it makes. For example, the word honk actually honks when you say it, and the word buzz imitates the sound of a bee. We can see this at work in the following excerpt from "Death of a Naturalist," by contemporary Irish poet Seamus Heaney (1939–).

Then one hot day when fields were rank
With cowdung in the grass the angry frogs
Invaded the flax-dam; I ducked through hedges
To a coarse croaking that I had not heard
Before. The air was thick with a bass chorus.
Right down the dam gross-bellied frogs were cocked
On sods; their loose necks pulsed like sails. Some hopped:
The slap and plop were obscene threats. Some sat
Poised like mud grenades, their blunt heads farting.
I sickened, turned, and ran. The great slime kings
Were gathered there for vengeance and I knew
That if I dipped my hand the spawn would clutch it.

This poem is rich with sounds, and the onomatopoetic words really stand out. We can hear the croaking, the hopping, the slap, and the plop. These sounds make the frogs in the poem come alive as they take over the dam and overwhelm the speaker.

Working with sounds, whether through alliteration, consonance, assonance, or onomatopoeia, can be fun and gives your poems a deeper emotional feeling. Paying attention to the music of individual words will help you pick words that breathe life into a moment, set a mood, and unleash emotions. No matter if you whisper or yell, your readers want to experience it, hearing the sounds.

Line breaks and stanza breaks are important tools that help people read poems as the writer intended them to be read. Think of line breaks and stanza breaks as the poet's special directions to you. When you write, you should use these breaks to match the way you read the poem.

Line breaks occur at the end of each line. Many poets write their thoughts in sentences, using a period at the end of the thought. However, these thoughts don't have to end at the end of a line. Lines can break after a word, phrase, or complete sentence. Poets have creative control over their line breaks and use them to produce different effects. Usually, line breaks give emphasis to the end of the line, and the break might be used to surprise readers with the next line. Readers typically pause a little at each line break, although the pause is usually shorter than the pause after a period.

You can see this emphasis and element of surprise at work in the poem "We Real Cool," by African-American poet Gwendolyn Brooks (1917–2000).

THE POOL PLAYERS.
SEVEN AT THE GOLDEN SHOVEL.

We real cool. We
Left school. We

WE REAL COOL

Lurk late. We
Strike straight. We

Sing sin. We
Thin gin. We

Jazz June. We
Die soon.

Brooks was inspired to write this poem after watching some school dropouts playing pool. By ending each line on we, she placed extra emphasis on the kids. Additionally, breaking the lines in the middle of sentences makes readers curious to read on.

Typically, line length tells readers how the poem should be read. Usually, a short line made up of only a few words tells readers to read slower, with more emphasis on each word. Even though there are more words in a long line, long lines are often read faster. In the poem "The Dance," American poet William Carlos Williams (1883–1963) uses longer lines and interesting line breaks to give motion to his poem.

THE DANCE

In Breughel's great picture, The Kermess,
the dancers go round, they go round and
around, the squeal and the blare and the
tweedle of bagpipes, a bugle and fiddles
tipping their bellies (round as the thick-
sided glasses whose wash they impound)
their hips and their bellies off balance
to turn them. Kicking and rolling about
the Fair Grounds, swinging their butts, those
shanks must be sound to bear up under such
rollicking measures, prance as they dance
in Breughel's great picture, The Kermess.

The rhythm and rhyme in the poem help give it motion; however, you probably feel this motion more because of Williams's line breaks in the middle of his thoughts and after less important words such as and, the, and such. The line breaks seem to emphasize the wild music of the poem, pulling your eye to the next line.

Stanza breaks are another important tool to help readers understand how to read a poem. Stanza breaks can be used to divide up the ideas or moments in a poem, and sometimes they are used to give poems a certain visual look. In most cases, you would treat the space between stanzas like a long pause. You can see how stanza breaks work in the poem "August," by contemporary American poet Mary Oliver (1935–).

AUGUST

When the blackberries hang
swollen in the woods, in the brambles
nobody owns, I spend

all day among the high
branches, reaching
my ripped arms, thinking

of nothing, cramming
the black honey of summer
into my mouth; all day my body

accepts what it is. In the dark
creeks that run by there is
this thick paw of my life darting among

the black bells, the leaves; there is
this happy tongue.

The stanza breaks in Oliver's poem help readers concentrate on each image and moment in the poem and create anticipation for the next stanza. For example, in the first stanza, she focuses on the blackberries, and then she breaks to a new stanza to focus on her action. Additionally, the word "thinking" at the end of the second stanza makes us hang there for a second, almost as if we are thinking for a moment ourselves. This pause heightens the anticipation for the next line and the next stanza.

When you work in form, there are more rules concerning line breaks and stanza breaks. However, when you write in free verse, you can play with lines and stanzas to achieve certain effects. Even though poems are meant to be heard, we usually share our poems with others by first writing or typing them on a page. So let your poems echo with rhyme, thump with rhythm, and celebrate sound. You have the power to make the music of your poem leap off the page.

STANZA BREAKS

1. Advice: Reading aloud. You'll get the most enjoyment out of a poem by reading aloud, but there are some important things to remember. First, don't rush. Try to feel and hear every word. Second, try to follow the poet's signals on the page. Line breaks tell readers to pause briefly, and stanza breaks tell readers to pause for a longer amount of time.

2. Recommended Resources: *Poetry Speaks.* Hearing a poet read aloud almost always gives you greater insight into a poem. At your library, ask for the Caedmon series of poetry recordings (on CD or tape). Additionally, the book *Poetry Speaks*, edited by Elise Paschen and Rebekah Presson Mosby, features biographies of poets and three CDs of the poets reading their works.

3. Activity: Line breaks. Take a paragraph from a newspaper or magazine. Now, if you were going to make this paragraph into a poem, where would you place the line breaks? What words would you give special emphasis? Where would you like readers to wait a second in suspense for the next line? Play with line breaks to see all of the different effects they can have.

4. Group Activity: Writing limericks. Gather a group of friends and have each person write the name of a city, town, or country on a scrap of paper and put it into a hat. Taking turns, pick a place and incorporate it into a limerick. Your poem should begin "There once was a _____ from ____." Look at Edward Lear's limerick on page 19 as an example to follow.

5. Activity: Neighborhood haiku. Haikus traditionally speak about nature. Take a walk around your neighborhood and observe the nature around you. Even if you live in a busy city, nature is present. Taking the images you observed, write a haiku that helps bring the moment to life. Haikus are three lines long and follow a five-seven-five syllable form.

6. Activity: End rhyme. Write a poem using end rhyme. First, try using perfect rhyme, like Robert Frost did in "Stopping by Woods on a Snowy Evening." Next, try using slant rhyme, similar to what Emily Dickinson did in "I Heard a Fly Buzz When I Died." Which type of rhyme do you like better? What is the effect of each type of rhyme?

7. Activity: Take the form challenge. Write a villanelle, using Theodore Roethke's villanelle as a model. The villanelle follows a strict rhyming pattern and is six stanzas long; the first five stanzas have three lines, and the sixth stanza has four. Many poets find it helpful to write the two repeating lines first. Be sure to share your finished villanelle with others. It's a big accomplishment!

8. Activity: Working with sound. Write a poem using alliteration, assonance, consonance, and ono-matopoeia. Pick sounds that emphasize the feeling in the poem. If it is a calming poem, try using l and s words. If it is an upbeat poem, try using the letters p and t. There are many other combinations that will give you certain effects, so just explore!

9. Recommended Resources: A rhyming dictionary. If you enjoy working with rhyme or are interested in writing more form poetry, you may find a rhyming dictionary helpful. Rhyming dictionaries show you the most common rhymes, but they also provide rhyme possibilities that are less common. *The Scholastic Rhyming Dictionary* by Sue Young is a good source for beginning poets.

10. Group Activity: Poetry reading. Organize a poetry reading. A few things to note: clap to welcome the reader, and clap after the person's reading. In addition, everyone should be absolutely quiet during each person's reading. Poetry readings are a great way to share your work with others, hear what friends are writing, and get new ideas for writing and improving your poems.

GLOSSARY

alliteration: the repetition of similar consonant sounds at the beginning of words, such as the l sound in lazy lonely lake

assonance: the repetition of similar vowel sounds in words, such as the long O sound in old stone road

consonance: the repetition of beginning and end consonant sounds in words, such as step/stop

contemporary: of the present time

free verse: a type of poetry that varies from the often strict rhymes, rhythms, and meters in form poetry

meter: a pattern of rhythms (accented syllables) in a line or entire poem

minstrel: a musician or singer from medieval times

Modern: a term applied to poets and poetry of the early 1900s and beyond; Modern poets tried to write poetry that was "new," breaking traditional rules

onomatopoeia: words that make the same sound as their name, such as chirp, pop, and bang

oral tradition: the practice of passing on information through the spoken word

rhyme: words that echo one another because of their similar sounds

rhyme scheme: a pattern of rhymes

rhythm: the sound of accents, or stresses, on syllables or words

sonnets: 14-line poems that follow a special form

stanza: a group of lines in a poem separated from other lines with white space

SELECTED WORKS

Brooks, Gwendolyn. *Selected Poems.* New York: HarperCollins, 1999.

Clifton, Lucille. *Blessing the Boats: New and Selected Poems, 1988–2000.* Rochester, New York: BOA Editions, 2000.

Dickinson, Emily. *The Collected Poems of Emily Dickinson.* New York: Random House, 1988.

Frost, Robert. *The Poetry of Robert Frost.* 2nd ed. New York: Henry Holt, 2002.

Heaney, Seamus. *Opened Ground: Selected Poems, 1966–1996.* New York: Farrar, Straus, and Giroux, 1999.

Lear, Edward. *A Book of Nonsense* (Everyman's Library Children's Classics Series). New York: Knopf, 1992.

Oliver, Mary. *New and Selected Poems.* Boston: Beacon Press, 2004.

Shakespeare, William. *The Sonnets.* New York: Penguin Classics, 2001.

Whitman, Walt. *Poems: Walt Whitman* (Everyman's Library Pocket Poets). New York: Knopf, 1994.

INDEX